FULFILLING THE MISSION

PURPOSEFUL DISCIPLESHIP

A 21-WEEK, 3-PART STUDY

STUDENT PIECE

ROLLAND & ELLEN DANIELS

Fulfilling the Mission: Purposeful Discipleship (Student Piece)
Written by Rolland and Ellen Daniels. We also want to mention those who made critical additional contributions to this study. Cal Bloom, Kris Bowers, and Fred Bays invested their hearts and insights into different aspects of it. Kris, in particular, contributed significantly to the Matters of the Heart section. We are indebted and grateful for each one's invaluable input.

Requests for information should be sent to:
Warner Press Inc.
P.O. Box 2499
Anderson, IN 46018
www.warnerpress.org

Kevin Stiffler and Liz Flinn • Editors
Curtis Corzine • Layout & Design
9781684346615

CONTENTS

INTRODUCTION

Fulfilling the Mission: Purposeful Discipleship was originally offered as three separate classes, with each successive class building on elements of the previous ones. They have been combined here for ease of use.

The entire study covers twenty-one weeks, with seven weeks per section. The first section, Foundations, focuses on the basics of the Christian faith; the second section, Building Bridges, focuses on connecting with others to share one's faith; and the third section, Matters of the Heart, focuses on deeper faith issues such as accountability and integrity. The entire course could be taught in one stretch, or you might take a week or two off between sections. Homework is a part of participating, and the course functions best as a "closed group"—that is, it will not work well for new students to join after the first week.

The Leader's Guide for *Fulfilling the Mission* can be found online at www.warnerpress.org/fulfillingthemission; it contains all content of the study, plus suggested answers to the questions and additional guidance for leading the group. Any Bible version could be used for completing the study, but quotations in the Student Piece and suggested answers in the Leader's Guide are based on the New International Version (NIV).

It is important for Christians to understand what they believe and why they believe it. The ultimate goal of this study is to provide a solid foundation for living out your faith, foster a conversational knowledge of your faith, and build confidence for sharing your faith with others. Enjoy the journey!

PART 1

FOUNDATIONS

1.1
INTRO WEEK

What can I expect from this study? What will a typical session look like? Will there be homework? What is discipleship? Does it have a relational aspect?

Basics for Belief Ground Rules

1. Remember the purpose of this segment of the study—to understand and help you more fully take hold of your relationship with God.
2. No question is too basic or silly—we learn *together.*
3. Basic assumption—the Bible is true (please bring a Bible).
4. Participate—add to the discussion and do your best to complete the work before your meeting time.
5. Let us know if you just do not like to read aloud or pray aloud. We will never intentionally put you in an uncomfortable position.
6. Be respectful of others and allow time for them to share.
7. As your leader shares answers, write them in your book. This is not cheating; we want you to have the answers.

Icebreaker Question

How long have you been coming to this church, and what are you hoping to gain from this study?

What to Expect During This First Segment of the Study

- To meet new friends and deepen old friendships.
- To gain knowledge.
- To understand your faith in a deeper, more fruitful way.
- To consider how to tell the story of Jesus.

What will a typical session look like?

- There will be a Memory Verse that goes along with each lesson. Focus on it during the week and do your best to memorize it before the next class, remembering that we are not looking for perfection.
- There will be work to do outside of our meeting time each week, including searching the Scriptures for answers. Be sure to come to class—even if you do not get your work done. Each week we will have time for feedback on the previous week's work.
- Additional Resources for digging further will often be offered; they are optional.

What is discipleship?

1. Discipleship is not something that makes us instantly Christian; it is a process of learning about Jesus and growing closer to him in a personal relationship.
2. Discipleship involves deep personal interaction with God's Word and purposeful interaction with Jesus himself that leads to a transformed life.
3. Discipleship is a time of learning and practicing right behaviors and right beliefs (core convictions).
4. There is a relational aspect to discipleship. It involves sharing life with others—the good and the bad, the easy/fun and the difficult.
5. You cannot share Christ effectively with people you do not know, so it is important to earn the right to be heard by first becoming a trusted friend, walking with people to help lead them to be fully devoted followers of Christ.

MEMORY VERSE

Matthew 28:19

HOMEWORK

1. If you have not already done so, write out the Memory Verse above. Memorize it before next week's meeting.
2. Review and complete Lesson 1.2 for next week.

Questions about anything?

Closing Prayer

1.2

WHO IS JESUS?

What does it mean to be a Christ-follower? Who is Jesus Christ? Why does he matter? What is unique about Christianity?

Feedback from Last Week's Homework

Review Memory Verse from Last Week—Matthew 28:19

Suggestions for Making Scripture Memory Successful:

1. ________________ the verse down many times during the week.
2. Say the verse ________________________—especially in front of others.
3. ________________ the verse with your spouse, children, or friends.
4. ________________ the verse somewhere obvious where you will see and read it often.

Crucial Points about Jesus ________________

Jesus' Humanity

- Philippians 2:3–5:

- Philippians 2:6–11:

- Hebrews 2:17–18:

Jesus' Divinity

- Colossians 1:15:

- Colossians 1:16:

- Colossians 1:17:

- Colossians 1:19:

The Benefits of Jesus Coming

- Luke 4:16–21:

- John 3:16:

- John 3:17:

- John 10:10:

Crucial Questions

1. Who is Jesus Christ, and why is Christianity unique?
   - John 14:6–7; John 3:16; 2 Timothy 3:16–17; 1 Corinthians 15:3–4:

2. Why did God send Jesus?
   - Luke 19:1–10:

3. Why did Jesus have to die?
   - 1 Peter 3:18; Isaiah 53:

4. What does Jesus' resurrection mean for me?
   - 1 Corinthians 15:17, 56–58:

5. How do I become a Christian?
   - Ephesians 2:8–9; Romans 3:21–28; Romans 10:9–10; 1 John 1:9:

Look up the references listed below. What do they reveal about Jesus?

- John 6:35:
- John 8:12:
- John 10:9:
- John 10:11:
- John 11:25:

- John 14:6:

- John 15:1:

What do these truths mean for my life?

Lee Strobel's book *The Case for Christ* (Grand Rapids: Zondervan, 1998) presents a powerful and time-tested argument supporting who Jesus is and what he did for us. Here are a few of the points Strobel makes:

- The Gospel writers based their information on eyewitness accounts. When the Gospels were written, there had been nowhere near enough time for verbal legends to develop.
- The manuscript evidence for the New Testament is solid, and there are numerous ancient sources that corroborate more than one hundred facts concerning Jesus' life, teachings, crucifixion, and resurrection.
- The New Testament confirms that Jesus is the only one in history who has matched the "fingerprint" of Messianic prophecies found in the Old Testament.
- The evidence from history, medicine, body mechanics, and the actions of Jesus' disciples following his time on this earth prove that his death and resurrection were no hoax.

MEMORY VERSE

John 14:6

HOMEWORK

1. If you have not already done so, write out the Memory Verse above. Memorize it before next week's meeting.
2. Check out the seven "I Am" claims of Jesus from John 1—3. This is a great section of Scripture that reveals a lot of who Christ really is.

3. Review and complete Lesson 1.3 for next week.

Additional Resources

- *The Case for Christ* by Lee Strobel (Grand Rapids: Zondervan, 1998)
- *The Road Less Traveled* by M. Scott Peck (New York: Random House, 1978)
- *Mere Christianity* by C. S. Lewis (London: Geoffrey Bles, 1952)

Closing Prayer

1.3

WHO IS GOD?

Who is God? How can we know about God? What is God like?

Feedback from Last Week's Homework

Review Memory Verse from Last Week—John 14:6

Crucial Questions

1. What was your first perception or understanding of God? How did you arrive at this understanding?

2. What can we learn about God through creation? What can we learn about God through his Word? How do each of these speak to you in different ways? (See Psalm 19.)

3. What are the attributes of God? What does each attribute mean for us?

- Genesis 1:1: God is ______________________
- Exodus 34:5–7: God is ______________________
- Romans 14:10: God is ______________________
- Isaiah 6:1–3: God is ______________________
- Acts 17:24: God is ______________________
- Isaiah 49:26: God is ______________________

Review the attributes of God above, then assess how or if Jesus represents those attributes by looking at the following verses and making notes about Jesus' attributes: Colossians 1:15–16; Mark 1:40–42; Mark 2:1–5; John 21:15–17; Romans 2:16; John 1:43–50; John 14:7; 2 Corinthians 5:21; Matthew 8:23–27; Ephesians 1:7:

4. How does John 14:9 indicate that Jesus has the same attributes as God?

5. What do the following verses say about the Trinity—God as three persons in one being?

- Romans 3:30:

- John 20:28; Romans 9:5; 2 Peter 1:1:

- Romans 8:9:

- 2 Corinthians 13:14:

6. Based on Psalm 139:1–3; Romans 3:23; and John 3:16, what is God's view of me?

MEMORY VERSE

Hebrews 11:6

HOMEWORK

1. If you have not already done so, write out the Memory Verse above. Memorize it before next week's meeting.
2. Take a look through Genesis 1—3 and the first chapter of John's Gospel and note what they reveal about God, Jesus, and the Holy Spirit.
3. Imagine you were to meet God and could ask him one question. What would it be?
4. Review and complete Lesson 1.4 for next week.

Additional Resources

- *Reaching for the Invisible God* by Philip Yancey (Grand Rapids: Zondervan, 2002)
- *Knowing God* by J. I. Packer (Downers Grove: InterVarsity Press, 1973)
- *A Room Called Remember* by Frederick Buechner (New York: Harper Collins, 1984)

Closing Prayer

1.4
DISCOVERING GOD'S WORD

What is the Bible about? Why is it important? How do I use it?

Feedback from Last Week's Homework

Review Memory Verse from Last Week—Hebrews 11:6

Crucial Questions

1. Why is the Bible important? Reflect on the following verses to answer this question:

- Hebrews 4:12–13:
- Psalm 119:105:
- 2 Timothy 3:16–17:

2. How should I use the Bible? Reflect on the following verses to answer this question:

- Romans 10:17:
- Nehemiah 8:8:
- Psalm 119:11:
- Psalm 119:15–16:
- Ezra 7:9–10:

Steps to Inductive Bible Study

1. *What?*

2. *So what?*

3. *Now what?*

MEMORY VERSE

Psalm 119:11

HOMEWORK

1. If you have not already done so, write out the Memory Verse above. Memorize it before next week's meeting.
2. Check out Genesis 22; 2 Kings 22—23; and Matthew 5—7 to see what they reveal about God's Word.
3. Set a goal to read from the Bible each day this week for at least ten minutes. How has God spoken to you from what you have read? How has it made a difference for you?

4. Begin to work on memorizing the order of the books of the Old and New Testaments. This will help you find your way around without having to always look at the table of contents.
5. Review and complete Lesson 1.5 for next week.

Additional Resources

- *The Bible Companion—A Handbook for Beginners* by Ronald D. Witherup (New York: The Crossroad Publishing Company, 1998)
- *What the Bible Is All About* by Henrietta C. Mears (Ventura: Regal Books, 1997)
- *How to Read the Bible for All Its Worth* by Gordon D. Fee and Douglas Stuart (Grand Rapids: Zondervan 1981)
- *52 Ways to Know Your Bible Better* by Robert Jon Crown (Nashville: Thomas Nelson, 1992)

Closing Prayer

1.5

THE HOLY SPIRIT

Who is the Holy Spirit? What does the Bible teach about the Holy Spirit? What does the Holy Spirit do?

Feedback from Last Week's Homework

Review Memory Verse from Last Week—Psalm 119:11

Crucial Questions

1. When did you first hear about the Holy Spirit?

2. What questions do you have about the Holy Spirit? In what ways do you struggle with the concept of the Holy Spirit?

3. Who is the Holy Spirit?

- John 14:16; Romans 8:26–27:

  Our ______________________________

- John 16:13; Romans 8:14; Acts 6:3:

  Our ______________________________

- Acts 9:31:

  Our ______________________________

4. You have considered who the Holy Spirit *is*; now think about what he *does*.

- John 14:17:
  The Holy Spirit ____________________________________

- Acts 2:38; 1 Corinthians 3:16:
  The Holy Spirit ____________________________________

- John 14:26; 16:12–14; 1 Corinthians 2:10–13:
  The Holy Spirit ____________________________________

- Galatians 5:16–25:
  The Holy Spirit ____________________________________

- Acts 1:8:
  The Holy Spirit ____________________________________

> **Read Acts 2:1–12.** Your church may be one that does not usually exercise some of the Spirit's gifts (such as tongues or prophecy) in public worship, seeing these gifts instead as something to be used in a person's prayer closet or private times of worship. Those who hold this view are comfortable with their own approach and do not take issue with those who choose to exercise these gifts in public settings. It is important that we do not limit the Holy Spirit to our finite human understanding.

5. How and when do we receive the Holy Spirit?

- Ephesians 1:13; 1 Corinthians 12:13:

MEMORY VERSE

John 14:26

HOMEWORK

1. If you have not already done so, write out the Memory Verse above. Memorize it before next week's meeting.
2. Take a look at John 16:5–16 to see what else you can learn about the Holy Spirit.
3. In what area of your life do you especially need the Holy Spirit to work right now?
4. Look for ways the Holy Spirit is already at work in your life. How do you sense the changes the Spirit is bringing about?
5. Review and complete Lesson 1.6 for next week.

Additional Resources

- *The Life You've Always Wanted* by John Ortberg (Grand Rapids: Zondervan, 2015)

Closing Prayer

1.6

DISCOVERING PRAYER

What is prayer? What words should I use? What kinds of things should I pray about? Will God answer my prayers? If so, how?

Feedback from Last Week's Homework

Review Memory Verse from Last Week—John 14:26

Crucial Questions

1. What is prayer—not the Facebook version where everything is perfect, but the real thing? Prayer is conversing (communicating) with God and offering him the following:

- Psalm 145:1–3:

- Psalm 100:4:

- Matthew 6:12; Hosea 14:1–7:

- Psalm 95:6–7:

- Philippians 4:6:

- Matthew 6:10:

Prayer is seeking ____________________, not his approval of ____________________.

Prayer is a privilege, not a duty, and is connected with the ongoing intercession of Christ for us at the right hand of God (Hebrews 10:1–25).

2. Why do we pray?
   - Psalm 34:17; 1 John 5:14:
   - 1 Peter 5:7; Luke 12:28:
3. Why does prayer matter?
   - James 5:16–18:
4. What is the ultimate "benefit" from prayer?
   - Romans 8:28:

Read Matthew 6:5–13. From verses 5–8, record what we can learn about prayer:

- Don't pray ____________________.
- Pray in __________________ and in __________________.
- Effective prayer is not about ____________________.
- God knows our ____________________.

From verses 9–13, record what you learn about God, Jesus, God's kingdom, faith, forgiveness, and temptation:

- God is our Father and deserves great ______________ and ______________ as we enter his presence.
- In Jesus coming there was a ______________ of heaven and earth; we are a part of his Kingdom work and ______________ his will right now.

- We should pray in faith that God will meet our ________________ and ________________ needs, not our wants; this also includes "bread" for our spiritual needs.
- We need to both ________________ and ________________ forgiveness; this includes confession.
- God will help to keep us from ________________ or ________________; but if we do face it, he will give us the courage, strength, and wisdom to prevail and live out our faith.

Here is a simple prayer pattern you can use, based on the acrostic ***ACTS***:

Adoration (telling God how you feel about him)
Confession (telling God where you have fallen short)
Thanksgiving (expressing appreciation to God for what he has done)
Supplication (seeking God's help for specific needs)

And to conclude your prayer times, be sure to *listen*.

5. What does prayer require?
- Matthew 6:5–6:
- Matthew 21:21–22:
- Matthew 6:7:

6. How are our prayers answered?
- "Yes."
- "No."
- "Wait."
- "I've got a better plan."

Practical Suggestions Regarding Prayer

- Matthew 6:7:

- Philippians 4:6:

- 1 John 5:14:

- Matthew 9:27–29:

- Luke 11:5–10:

MEMORY VERSE

Philippians 4:6

HOMEWORK

1. If you have not already done so, write out the Memory Verse above. Memorize it before next week's meeting.
2. Read from the Psalms (choose a variety), Ephesians 3:14–21 (read it out loud), and John 17 to see what you learn about prayer.
3. Set a goal to stop and pray each day this week for at least ten minutes. You might also begin a journal by writing out your prayers, noting any specific answers to your prayers. This will serve as a reminder of God's faithfulness to you as you look back. What answers have you seen to your prayers? How have they made a difference for you?

4. Review and complete Lesson 1.7 for next week. And have fun with it! You will be briefly writing out your faith story. If you have done this previously, you might pull out your old version and update/revise/review it. Be comfortable with it and consider scenarios when you might tell just certain portions of your story as your audience changes.

Additional Resources

- *100 Prayers for Making Faith Connections*, ed. by John van Bemmel (Notre Dame, IN: Ave Maria Press, 1999)
- *Teach Me to Pray* by Andrew Murray (Uhrichsville, OH: Barbour Publishing, 1982)

Closing Prayer

1.7

MY STORY

How can I tell others about Jesus and my story of faith?

Feedback from Last Week's Homework

Review Memory Verse from Last Week—Philippians 4:6

It is time to start writing out your faith story. You will begin by taking time to recall and reflect on important moments and events in your life, helping you create a timeline to "tell your story." You can include as much or as little as you desire in this timeline, but the more time you spend on it, the easier and more natural the crux of your faith story will become to share with others.

On a separate piece of paper, complete these items:

1. Briefly summarize the details below on a timeline continuum. Begin with the year of your birth, and end with your death—obviously an unknown date in the future. In the in-between spaces, add some or all of the following. There are no rules—this is *your* story! Include what you want, even events or memories not on this list:

- Important/meaningful life events
  - Birth of siblings
  - Great vacations/memories
  - First job
  - Awards won or achievements earned
- Negatives in your life
  - Loss of a pet
  - Friend moved away
  - Parent moved out

    - Death of a loved one
    - Divorce
    - Loss of a job
- "Mountaintop" spiritual experiences—anything that caused great joy or growth
    - Camps, retreats, vacation Bible school
    - How and when you were introduced to church
    - A class, book, or Bible study that was especially meaningful
    - When spiritually influential people entered your life
    - Date when and how you accepted Christ

2. Now divide your timeline into three sections:
    - My life before I met Christ
    - When/how I met Christ (this will be a moment in time)
    - My life after I met Christ

3. As you ponder the three different sections of your timeline, think about how you felt during each section. Remember, your conversion story may not be an overly dramatic, 360-degree turnaround, flash-of-lightning-type of experience. In other words, your life before meeting Christ may have been pretty mellow, and your life after having met Christ may simply be a series of growth steps to be more like him rather than a seemingly instantaneous phenomenal change. Both are wonderful stories.

Share your story's highlights with another person or two in the class, in no longer than three minutes if possible. Continue to think about your story and become comfortable with it, knowing that it will be added to throughout your life as God allows opportunities and experiences that grow your faith and help you become more like Christ. We will work even more on our faith stories in the next section, Building Bridges. The more comfortable we get telling our stories, the more natural our sharing becomes. And then it is "not about us," but rather about God in us.

PART 2

BUILDING BRIDGES

2.1
INTRO WEEK

What can I expect in this section? How can I begin to build bridges for Christ with those in my life? How can I be ready to share Christ when the time is right?

Building Bridges Ground Rules

1. Remember the purpose of this segment of the study—to grow your confidence in sharing your faith journey with others. Begin praying now about whom you can share with.
2. No question is too basic or silly—we learn *together.*
3. Basic assumption—you have accepted Christ as your Savior. (If not, please share with your group leader.)
4. Participate—add to the discussion and do your best to complete the work before your meeting time.
5. Let us know if you just do not like to read aloud or pray aloud. We will never intentionally put you in an uncomfortable position.
6. Be respectful of others and allow time for them to share.
7. As your leader shares answers, write them in your book. This is not cheating; we want you to have the answers.

Icebreaker Question

What has your discipleship journey been like thus far (am a new believer, have been a Christian for years but never participated in discipleship, have been in Bible studies before, etc.)?

What to Expect During This Second Segment of the Study

- To continue deepening relationships with other group members.
- To continue better understanding your faith.

- To become familiar with how to tell the story of Jesus.
- To continue growing more comfortable with sharing about your faith.
- To intentionally begin sharing Jesus with others.

What will a typical session look like?

- There will be a Memory Verse that goes along with each lesson. Focus on it during the week and do your best to memorize it before the next class, remembering that we are not looking for perfection.
- There will be work to do outside of our meeting time each week, including searching the Scriptures for answers. Be sure to come to class—even if you do not get your work done. Each week we will have time for feedback on the previous week's work.
- Additional Resources for digging further will often be offered; they are optional.

A Review of the Nature of Discipleship

1. Discipleship is not a process that makes us instantly Christian; it is a process of learning about Jesus and growing closer to him in a personal relationship.
2. Discipleship involves deep personal interaction with God's Word and purposeful interaction with Jesus himself that leads to a transformed life.
3. Discipleship is a time of learning and practicing right behaviors and right beliefs (core convictions).
4. There is a relational aspect to discipleship. It involves sharing life with others—the good and the bad, the easy/fun and the difficult.
5. You cannot share Christ effectively with people you do not know, so it is important to earn the right to be heard by first becoming a trusted friend, walking with people to help lead them to be fully devoted followers of Christ.

MEMORY VERSE

Acts 5:42

HOMEWORK

1. If you have not already done so, write out the Memory Verse above. Memorize it before next week's meeting.
2. Think of three people in your life you are in regular contact with who are not believers:

   Ask God to help you build a closer relationship with these people, and begin praying daily for them.
3. Review and complete Lesson 2.2 for next week.

Questions about anything?

Closing Prayer

2.2

DISCOVERING GOD'S GUIDANCE

How do I know what God wants? What kinds of decisions does God care about? How do I discern God's voice?

Feedback from Last Week's Homework

Review Memory Verse from Last Week—Acts 5:42

Crucial Questions

1. Of the three questions below, which is most important to you and why?
   - How do I know what God wants?
   - How should I approach talking to God in prayer?
   - How do I discern God's voice among all the other voices speaking into my life?

2. How do I know what God wants?
   - James 1:5:
   - Proverbs 2:1–11:

3. How should I approach talking to God in prayer?
   - Philippians 4:6–7:
   - Psalm 37:1–5:

- Hebrews 4:15–16:

4. All of us have multiple voices that speak to us on various subjects. No wonder it is sometimes difficult to discern what is right and who is really telling the truth. How do I discern God's voice from all the other voices speaking into my life?
   - Isaiah 26:3–4:
   - 1 Kings 19:9–12:
   - 1 John 4:1–2:
5. As believers, where does our guidance come from?
   - Psalm 32:8; 119:105:
   - John 14:15–17:
   - Proverbs 15:22:
   - Psalm 77:10–11:
   - Proverbs 2:1–12:
6. What does it mean when God is silent?
   - God sees what ____________________.
   - Sometimes God changes us before ____________________.
   - God's ways ____________________.
   - With God, a day is like ____________________.

MEMORY VERSE

James 1:5

HOMEWORK

1. If you have not already done so, write out the Memory Verse above. Memorize it before next week's meeting.
2. Look at Proverbs 3—4 and Acts 8:26–40 for some clues about discovering God's guidance in our lives.
3. Consider a time when you had to make an important decision. How did you decide? Was God a part of your decision? How might you choose differently now?
4. Look for ways God is at work in your life now. How are you at peace with him? What do you sense he is telling you?
5. Pray specifically each day this week about the three non-believers God brought to your mind. Ask God for opportunities to arise for initiating conversations about faith.
6. Review and complete Lesson 2.3 for next week.

Additional Resources

- *Experiencing God* by Henry T. Blackaby and Claude V. King (Nashville: B&H Publishing, 2008)

Closing Prayer

2.3

LIVING FOR GOD DAY BY DAY

Why do I face temptation? How should I respond to temptation?
What are the differences in my life now?
What if I don't "feel" any different?

Feedback from Last Week's Homework

Review Memory Verse from Last Week—James 1:5

Crucial Questions

1. How is my life different in Christ?
   - 2 Corinthians 5:17:

2. Temptations
   - 1 Corinthians 10:13; James 1:2–4, 13–15:

3. Emotions
   - Galatians 5:22–23; 1 John 5:11–13:

4. Balance
   - Luke 2:52:

A BALANCED LIFE

Based on Luke 2:52

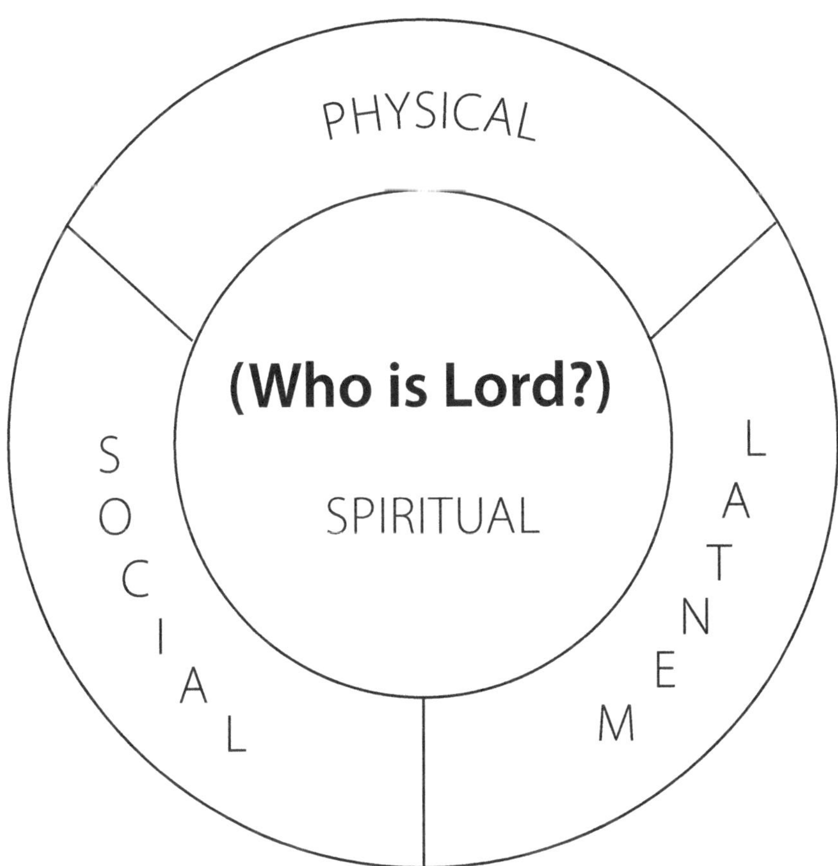

5. How is my stewardship (of time, money, and talents) different?

   Trust

   - Malachi 3:10; Matthew 6:19–21:

   Discipline

   - 2 Corinthians 9:7–8; 1 Corinthians 16:2:

6. What happens when we fail?

   - 1 John 1:8–10:

7. How do I strengthen my walk with the Lord?

   Ephesians 6:10–18: Put on ____________________

   - The belt of ____________________
   - The breastplate of ____________________
   - Feet fitted with the ____________________
   - The shield of ____________________
   - The helmet of ____________________
   - The sword of the ____________________

MEMORY VERSE

1 John 5:13

HOMEWORK

1. If you have not already done so, write out the Memory Verse above. Memorize it before next week's meeting.
2. Take a look at Genesis 39; the Book of Job; Matthew 4:1–11; and Colossians 3:1—4:6 for more about living for God day by day.

3. What is the toughest temptation you are facing right now? How are you letting God help you find a way out? Pray to see the way out this week and watch what happens.

4. How will you begin the path of stewardship we discussed today (time, money, talents)? What steps must you take to start this journey?

5. Pray for specific opportunities/encounters with the three non-believers God brought to your mind. Be watching and ready—God will answer your prayer.
6. Review and complete Lesson 2.4 for next week.

Additional Resources

- *There's a Snake in My Garden* by Jill Briscoe (Grand Rapids: Zondervan, 1980)

Closing Prayer

2.4

RELATING TO AND SERVING OTHERS

How can I forgive others and show love to them? How can I reach out to people who don't know God? How can I serve?

Feedback from Last Week's Homework

Review Memory Verse from Last Week—1 John 5:13

Crucial Questions

1. Discovering How to Relate to Others (Building Relationships)
   - John 15:12–13:
   - Colossians 3:13:
   - Proverbs 12:22:
   - 1 Corinthians 4:2:
   - Philippians 2:3–4:
2. Relationship Barriers
   - James 4:1–2; Proverbs 28:25:
   - Luke 12:16–20; Proverbs 16:18:
   - Job 5:2; Colossians 3:13:

3. Serving Wherever You Go—Four Keys:
    1. Commit yourself to care for others (Philippians 2:3–5):

    2. Position yourself to be available (Matthew 5:13–16):

    3. Live with integrity and character (Titus 2:7):

    4. Act on behalf of others (James 2:26; 3:13):

MEMORY VERSE

John 13:34–35

HOMEWORK

1. If you have not already done so, write out the Memory Verse above. Memorize it before next week's meeting.
2. Read Luke 15:11–32 and 1 Corinthians 13 to discover more about relating to and serving others.

3. Complete the online Spiritual Gifts Assessment listed below under Additional Resources, or another assigned by your group leader.
4. Think of someone or a group in your community that you or your study group could impact for the good of Jesus. What would it take to begin this work?

5. This week, spend time in prayer regarding healthy relationships in your life and ask God what barriers you may be placing between yourself and others.
6. Pray for God to open up further opportunities and encounters with the three non-believers he brought to your mind. Pray specifically. Be watching intently. And act when those God-moments happen.
7. Review and complete Lesson 2.5 for next week.

Additional Resources

- Spiritual Gifts Assessment: https://gifts.churchgrowth.org/spiritual-gifts-survey/

Closing Prayer

2.5

BUILDING RELATIONSHIPS FOR THE KINGDOM

Why is it important to take my faith "outside"?
How can I do that each day?

Feedback from Last Week's Homework

Review Memory Verse from Last Week—John 13:34–35

Crucial Questions

Six Steps to Sharing about Christ:

1. Remember that availability is the key (Acts 8:26):

2. Become spiritually sensitive with respect to your everyday life (Acts 8:27–29):

3. Intentionally build relationships with people (Acts 8:30):

4. Pray daily and be open to talking about spiritual things (Acts 8:31):

5. Know how to pray for unbelievers (1 Timothy 2:1–4; 1 John 4:7–8; 2 Corinthians 10:4–5):

6. Share your story (1 Peter 3:15):

MEMORY VERSE

Acts 1:8

HOMEWORK

1. If you have not already done so, write out the Memory Verse above. Memorize it before next week's meeting.
2. Look at Mark 6:30–44 and Ephesians 2:10 for more on building relationships for God's kingdom.
3. Pray specifically for the three non-believers God brought to your mind, asking him to strengthen you to step out in faith and be bold in witnessing to them.
4. Write out your story in Christ as instructed in Lesson 2.6 for next week. Start early in the week, pray for guidance, and express your heart honestly. Then review, revise, and get familiar with your story. You might possibly even practice sharing it with a trusted friend.

Additional Resources

- www.peacewithgod.net
- *Lifestyle Evangelism* by Joe Aldrich (Colorado Springs: Multnomah, 2006)
- *The Unchurched Next Door* by Thom S. Rainer (Grand Rapids: Zondervan, 2008)

Closing Prayer

2.6

TELLING MY STORY

Can I share my faith? How do I tell my story? What is the goal of sharing my story?

Feedback from Last Week's Homework

Review Memory Verse from Last Week— Acts 1:8

Crucial Questions

It's time to share!

Stories are powerful tools of communication. Our stories help others see how Jesus can give them hope and a transformed life. Below are some suggestions to help you tell your story in a concise way.

1. Describe your life before Christ (including your unsatisfied inner need). What were things like before you knew Jesus? In what ways did you lack peace or deep joy?
   - Did you attend church?
   - Were you raised in a Christian home?
   - Were both parents in the home, or was there a divorce or some other situation?

2. Describe the circumstances surrounding how you met Christ:
   - Was anyone instrumental in helping you?
   - Were you in church, at church camp or a retreat, or somewhere else?

- Did someone counsel you or pray with you?

3. Describe your life after meeting Christ (clarify how Jesus changed your life and what that change is like). What are things like now that you have met Jesus? We know things are not always perfect, but in what ways is your life different?

- More peace?
- More joy?
- More deep-seated happiness?
- Less worry?
- Less bitterness taking root?
- Less comparison to others who seemingly have it all?

Remember, there are no "right" or "best" answers. You are simply describing your story.

Suggestions for Sharing Your Story

- Remember that no two stories are exactly alike. God can and will use your own unique experiences to speak to others. Be real. Be authentic. Be yourself.
- Avoid using Christian clichés and jargon. Many words or phrases used in the church are confusing to unbelievers (for example: *sanctified, washed in the blood, propitiation, conversion,* etc.). Make an effort to translate "Christianese" into everyday language.

- Avoid dogmatic and controversial statements or subjects. Don't focus on topics that will probably turn off your listener.
- Don't use your story to criticize other churches, individuals, or groups.
- Don't try to be too dramatic or share shocking details from before you met Christ. Don't recite a laundry list of prior sinful behavior. Be discreet.
- Practice sharing your story with another believer to get more comfortable telling it. Try to be able to share it *in three minutes or less.*
- Before sharing your story, pray for God's divine power to make your story a part of God's work in transforming another's life. No two times you share your story will be the same.

One Method of Asking for a Decision: *God's Love for Us*

- The verses listed below are ones to familiarize yourself with, but don't feel you must have each one memorized before you can share:

1. John 3:16:

2. Romans 3:23:

3. Romans 6:23:

4. Romans 5:8:

5. Ephesians 2:8–9:

6. John 1:12:

7. Stop to ask if the person has any questions, would like to receive this gift, and would like to pray. If appropriate, lead the person in repeating prayer sentences after you: thanking God for his gift of

forgiveness and eternal life, confessing sin, and proclaiming Jesus Christ as Savior and Lord.

8. Remind the person that our faith is based on facts, not feelings. If we are trusting Christ for salvation then we are saved, even in those moments when it may not "feel" like it (see 1 John 1:9).
9. Encourage the person to follow up on her or his new decision by sharing the news with someone, or by setting a date the following week to meet with you again to discuss this decision.

Another Method of Asking for a Decision: The Roman Way or *A B C*

- This is a shorter approach and can be concluded with the same type of prayer. It is referred to as the "Roman Way," since it uses Romans 3:23; 6:23; 5:8; and 10:9–10:

  A: *Admit* your need.

  B: *Believe* in Jesus.

  C: *Confess* your wrongs.

Recapping some basics to remember when sharing Christ:

1. Be yourself.
2. Build a relationship.
3. Believe God can use you.
4. Remember, it is God's job to "save" people, not yours. You are only called to share about God's deep love and his desire for each person to know Jesus as Savior and Lord.

MEMORY VERSE

Matthew 10:32–33

HOMEWORK

1. If you have not already done so, write out the Memory Verse above. Memorize it before next week's meeting.
2. Read John 9 and note what it says about the difference Jesus made in one man's life.

3. Continue reviewing your story to build your confidence. Make certain you can share it in three minutes or less.
4. Continue practicing sharing your story. Ask trusted friends for suggestions to make it clearer and more concise. We will share our stories next week in class.
5. Pray specifically about when and with which of the three non-believers God brought to your mind you could share your faith story. Plan a time to do it, praying first for God's timing and for wisdom. Then watch what happens!

Additional Resources

- *Corner Conversations* by Randy Newman (Grand Rapids: Kregel Publications, 2011)

Closing Prayer

2.7
PRACTICE TELLING MY STORY

Feedback from Last Week's Homework

Review Memory Verse from Last Week—Matthew 10:32–33

This week will be a fun celebration of what we have learned about sharing Christ with others. We will also celebrate our growth in our knowledge of Christ, growth in our relationships with Christ, and growth in our confidence to share our stories.

This meeting is an opportunity for everyone in the study to share. We will take the whole time to share our stories. We may do some role playing to get started. We may also practice in pairs first. But we want to make sure to allow enough time for all to publicly share with the class.

Remember to continue to pray specifically for the three people God has brought to your mind and heart. Also remember to set a prayerful priority to share with at least one of these three people soon. Ask God to help you discern the "right time."

PART 3

MATTERS OF THE HEART

3.1

ACCOUNTABILITY, INTEGRITY, AND FINANCIAL RESPONSIBILITY

Matters of the Heart Ground Rules

1. Remember the purpose of this segment of the study—to go deeper in your relationship with Christ, specifically in your integrity and character as you live life.
2. No question is too basic or silly—we learn *together.*
3. Basic assumption—you are committed to growing as a disciple of Jesus.
4. Participate—add to the discussion and do your best to complete the work before your meeting time.
5. Let us know if you just do not like to read aloud or pray aloud. We will never intentionally put you in an uncomfortable position.
6. Be respectful of others and allow time for them to share.
7. As your leader shares answers, write them in your book. This is not cheating; we want you to have the answers.

Write *your* definition of integrity (not something you find online):

Now, using a dictionary or online resource, look up a definition of integrity and record what you find:

Read 1 Timothy 4:15–16. In verse 15, Paul told Timothy to "be diligent…so that everyone may see your progress." What was he trying to communicate?

In verse 16, Paul explained why integrity is important for leaders. What did he say?

Paul's teaching helps us understand why integrity is important for leaders. Now let's explore how the Bible defines integrity and compare it to the definitions you wrote and researched.

Read Matthew 23, where Jesus discussed ethics, morality, and integrity. We might differentiate between ethics and morality by defining ethics as one's "defined standard" of right and wrong—what a person believes—and morality as one's "lived standard" of right and wrong—how a person actually lives. To have integrity means that a person's ethics and morality are integrated, that they match (see *The Leadership Bible*, K. Boa and B. Perkins, eds. [Grand Rapids: Zondervan, 1998]).

We are all human and no person on earth lives completely aligned with a high and holy ethic. In what ways are your ethics and morality not integrated? Where do you see opportunities to grow? Where are you hypocritical in your life?

Read Psalm 139:23. What was David asking of God?

Read the following Bible passages and determine how accountability is to be used:

- 1 Samuel 13:5–13:
- Galatians 2:14:
- Romans 14:15–16:

Do you have true accountability in your life or only the appearance of accountability? Who holds you accountable? How often do you open yourself up for genuine accountability? In what areas of your life is accountability lacking?

Read 2 Samuel 12:1–14. Nathan was in the position of holding David, one of the greatest leaders for God, accountable for his sins. How did Nathan approach the situation? How did David respond? How did Nathan reassure David?

As leaders, we are sometimes in the position of having to hold someone accountable. How will you approach this? What do we learn from Nathan's interaction with David?

Being accountable to God means also being financially responsible. The Bible does talk a lot about things such as prayer and faith, but it actually addresses money and possessions much more frequently. Money is mentioned over two thousand times in the Scriptures. Jesus talked about money often, and a good portion of the New Testament relates to financial issues.

Why do you think there is such an emphasis in the Bible on money?

Acts 11:27–30 describes an offering given by the early disciples. According to this passage, what was its purpose?

In Genesis 14:20, Abram (who later became known as Abraham) gave God a tithe, or tenth, of his possessions. According to Leviticus 27:30–32, Old Testament law commanded God's people to tithe to the Lord. This practice continued in New Testament times. What does Matthew 22:15–22 imply about tithing?

What do Exodus 35:21–22 and Luke 16:10–11 indicate about our giving to God?

Malachi 3:8 states that the failure to give tithes and offerings is the equivalent of robbing God. Does this seem reasonable to you? Why or why not?

Read Luke 12:34. If someone examined your financial records, where might that person determine your heart to be? Remember, our spending determines our priorities:

How does your attitude toward money affect your personal relationship with God? Is giving a burden or a blessing, a duty or a privilege? Are you stingy or a steward? Why do you say so?

Our attitude toward money is shaped by our culture, both the culture we grew up in and our current culture. And as spiritual leaders, our stewardship choices influence the people we lead. What is the way you use money saying to those you lead in your home?

How about in your circles of influence both inside and outside of church?

Would you be comfortable sharing your financial decisions and day-to-day money management with others? Would others view you as living a financially responsible life? Why or why not?

Spiritual Growth Plan Reflection

1. Drawing from your responses to this lesson, list two or three actions you will take to work toward a more integrated life and strengthen your integrity.

2. Also list two or three actions you will take to invite others to hold you accountable for leading an integrated life.

3. Finally, list some actions you will take to hold those you lead accountable.

4. If you don't currently tithe, what steps will you take to move toward tithing? If you do tithe, what steps will you take to be more generous with God and others?

5. What do you want your financial lifestyle to say to others about your faith and your priorities?

Closing Prayer

3.2

RELATIONAL INTEGRITY AND CONFLICT MANAGEMENT

God created us to live in community with others, but it is not always easy. Our relationships are important to God. Read the following Bible passages and note what they say about God's vision for our relationships:

- John 17:22–23:
- Mark 12:28–31:
- 1 John 4:7, 11, 20–21:

Our friends shape our lives, bringing us encouragement from God and loving us even when we are difficult to love. Friendships also give us chances to both give and receive love and grace.

Make a list of some significant friendships or relationships in your life:

Read the following Bible passages and make a note of what each says about relationships:

- Ecclesiastes 4:9–12:
- Exodus 17:9–13:
- Colossians 3:12–17:

- Acts 2:42–47:

The emphasis on individualism in our culture tends to push us away from the deep and fruitful relationships described in the Scriptures, especially the prevalence of technology and the use of texting rather than experiencing face-to-face communication. The prevailing attitude that we have the freedom to do whatever we want, that we can do it ourselves without help, is detrimental to the relational life God desires for us. How does this cultural attitude affect your relationships?

How do you feel this type of living may impact the next generation?

What can you do about the above to make a difference?

Read the following Bible passages for insights about overcoming such an attitude:

- Matthew 23:11–12:

- Matthew 20:25–28:

- 1 Peter 5:5:

Conflict is a natural result of human relationships. As a Christ-follower, you will face relational conflicts and will need to manage them in a godly manner when they arise. In a famous sermon based on Matthew 5:43–45, Dr. Martin Luther King Jr. identified three principles of Jesus' admonition to love our enemies:

1. Develop and maintain the capacity to forgive. This doesn't mean ignoring a wrong committed against us, rather that we will not allow the wrong to be a barrier to the relationship.

2. Recognize that the wrong we suffer is not entirely representative of the other person's identity. We all have both good and bad qualities; we all have good and bad days.
3. Do not seek to defeat or humiliate those who wrong us, but instead to win their friendship and understanding. This is possible when God's unconditional love flows through us (see *The Leadership Bible)*.

Read Matthew 18:15–17 for a blueprint for dealing with conflict. Write down the steps to conflict management in your own words:

1.

2.

3.

4.

The Scriptures instruct us not only about the steps of conflict management, but also about our attitude when dealing with conflict. Read the following passages and note the attitude we are to have when managing conflict and the reason we should have this attitude:

- Ephesians 4:1–3:

- Philippians 2:3–4:

Read Matthew 5:23–25. What was Jesus talking about in this passage?

A basic part of loving others is practicing forgiveness. When we do so, we grow beyond our pain rather than being trapped in it as victims. Forgiving someone is as much for our own benefit as it is for the benefit of the other person. Jesus provided us with a clear example of forgiveness.

Read Mark 14:66–72. Describe the wrong done to Jesus by Peter:

Read John 21:15–19. Describe Jesus' method of communicating his forgiveness to Peter:

Read Acts 2:14–40. Who was speaking here, and what was he speaking about?

Spiritual Growth Plan Reflection

1. Identify broken relationships in your life that need attention and keep you and others from growing in a relationship with God. How are you going to manage these conflicts and arrive at a place of forgiveness? As a follower of Christ, how will you help others manage relationships and relational conflict?

2. Remember that not everyone is ready to discuss or work through conflict. But, as far as you are able, seek to deal with your conflicts so they are not a barrier to your spiritual growth. You cannot dictate how others will respond to your desire to heal broken relationships, but you can make an effort to bring healing.

Closing Prayer

3.3
CONFRONTING THE SHADOW SIDE

What prevents you from looking more like Jesus, which is our authentic mission as believers? Author and pastor John Ortberg talks about our "shadow mission," the unworthy, dark, self-centered tendencies that can quickly deteriorate our lives if not confronted. Ortberg suggests that our shadow mission is subtle. It is closely related to our gifts, abilities, passions, and calling. It's not 180 degrees off from our mission, but a subtle ten degrees off, making it much more difficult to identify (see *Overcoming Your Shadow Mission* [Grand Rapids: Zondervan, 2008]).

Read Matthew 19:16–22; Mark 10:17–30; and Luke 18:18–23. How do these passages describe the rich young man? How did he outwardly appear to be "good"?

What was this man's shadow mission, and how did it impact his relationship with God?

The Old Testament provides an example that contrasts with that of the rich young man. Take a look at the Book of Esther. From 3:1–11 and 4:1–11, what did Esther's shadow mission seem to be?

After being challenged by Mordecai, Esther said no to her shadow mission. Look at 5:1–8 and 7:1–4. What did she do instead?

Esther said no to a shadow mission of safety and security and yes to her authentic mission. Our authentic mission is always one of serving, to serve God's purposes on earth. In our culture, the shadow mission of "more" is prevalent—more wealth, power, applause, status, and recognition.

What is *your* shadow mission? What is it that, apart from the help of God, you tend to drift to?

Read the following passages. What does each one tell us about the shadow mission we may have?

- Luke 16:14–15:
- 1 Corinthians 4:5:
- 1 Thessalonians 2:1–4:

What does it look like for us to be authentically engaged in living life as God intends? Read Matthew 5—7, which recounts Jesus' famous Sermon on the Mount. As you read, list the standards of lifestyle you find that give us a picture of the life we *should* live, the life we *will* live when we allow the Holy Spirit to work in us:

Which of these lifestyle standards are difficult for you? In which of these areas are you living a shadow mission rather than your authentic mission?

Read Romans 5:6–8. What does this say about God's heart for us, even when we are on our shadow mission?

Spiritual Growth Plan Reflection

1. One reason Esther was able to say no to her shadow side and accept her authentic mission was because Mordecai challenged her. Who is the "Mordecai" in your life? Whom do you rely on to challenge you when you are off track?

   If you cannot name a "Mordecai" in your life, begin praying about who that person might be. We can all benefit from accountability and truth-tellers in our lives.

2. What is your authentic mission? How is it that God wants you to serve his purpose on earth?

3. What steps will you take to move away from your shadow mission and toward your authentic mission?

Closing Prayer

3.4
SEXUAL INTEGRITY

Why did God create sex? Read the following Bible passages and note what each says about why God created sex:

- Genesis 1:28:
- Genesis 2:24:
- Genesis 4:1:
- 1 Corinthians 7:2, 5:
- 2 Samuel 12:24:

What is a common thread that runs through each of the above passages as they describe why God created sex?

Clearly, God gave us sex to be enjoyed between a husband and wife in a committed marriage relationship. Why does God intend that sex be reserved for marriage?

How does sexual impurity affect our lives in each of these areas?

- Current relationships:

- Future relationships:

- Health:

- Self-image:

God is very clear about living righteously, especially in the area of sexuality. Read 1 Corinthians 6:9–20 and 1 Thessalonians 4:3–7 and note the reasons why sexual purity is so important to God:

The reality is that each one of us will be sexually tempted, but there are some specific ways God has equipped us to avoid sexual temptation.

Read 1 Corinthians 10:12–13. What does this passage say about how God will help us avoid temptation?

Reach the following passages and note what each says about how we can fight temptation:

- 2 Corinthians 10:3–5:

- Philippians 4:8:

- James 1:13–15:

For those who are married, the Scriptures provide another avenue for fighting sexual temptation. Read Proverbs 5:15–20. Husbands and wives, how can you enhance sex in your marriage?

Spiritual Growth Plan Reflection

1. The following is adapted from *Personal Holiness in Times of Temptation* by Bruce H. Wilkinson (Colorado Springs: Multnomah Books, 2001). Take time to walk through the following points and answer the questions.

   Victory comes through guarding your "temptability quotient." Our weaknesses become ways for Satan to tempt us. When we are feeling weak spiritually, physically, mentally, or emotionally, we are more vulnerable to temptation. Weariness makes for weakness. If we are aware of feeling weak, then we can guard against temptation. Are you feeling strong or weak spiritually? physically? mentally? emotionally? In what ways?

   Victory comes through breaking your temptation patterns. We often have patterns of behavior that leave us more vulnerable to temptation. Are there certain days of the week or times of the day when you are most tempted? Where are you and who is with you when you are most tempted? For example, when you are at home alone working on your computer, are you tempted to view pornography? Think about your daily habits and identify your temptation patterns:

Victory comes through practicing holiness habits. When we engage in behavior that draws us closer to God, we can more easily fight temptation. How often are you praying and reading the Bible? How often are you allowing others to hold you accountable? How much time and effort are you investing in serving the Lord and serving others?

Victory comes through turning temptations into triumphs. What are you going to do when you feel tempted? Who are you going to tell for accountability? How are you going to turn to God to help you overcome the temptation?

2. Remember that it is important to be ready when temptations come. You can do so by being proactive and having a plan in place.

Closing Prayer

3.5
SERVANTHOOD

With respect to being an effective servant leader, author R. K. Greenleaf wrote that such leaders take care to make other people's needs their highest priority, with the goal of helping others grow as persons by serving them in ways that lead to them become more healthy, more free, more wise, and more likely to become servants themselves (see *Servant Leadership: A Journey into the Nature of Legitimate Power & Greatness* [Mahwah, NJ: Paulist Press, 2002], 27).

Read John 13:1–17. How do the actions of Jesus in this passage connect with Greenleaf's definition of an effective servant leader?

Pay attention to verse 15 from the above passage. Why did Jesus command his disciples to do "as" he had done, rather than to do "what" he had done?

Read the following passages and note some concepts from each that further emphasize the nature of Jesus' servant leadership:

- Philippians 2:5–7:
- Matthew 20:28:
- Isaiah 53:4–5:

Read Mark 9:33–37. How does this biblical view of leadership differ from an approach to leadership that is based on "works" (performing right actions)?

From your experience, is the biblical view of leadership reflected in the world? Why or why not?

Read the following Bible passages and note the ways in which servant leadership is developed:

- Hebrews 5:7–10:
- Luke 2:41–47:
- 1 Timothy 5:
- Philippians 2:19–24:

Jesus is the ultimate model of servanthood, but one that is sometimes difficult for us to consider emulating. Read Acts 4:36–37 and 15:36–39 for a glimpse into the life of another servant leader in the Bible. What did Barnabas do in each of these situations? How did he exhibit servant leadership?

Leadership expert John Maxwell stipulates that leaders can select one of two opposing orientations toward their organizations. The first approach is to take from the organization whatever benefits can be obtained. The other approach us to consider what he or she can give or contribute to the organization (see *The Maxwell Leadership Bible* [Nashville: Thomas Nelson, 2002], 1,259). Using this concept and the examples of Jesus and Barnabas, take a few minutes to reflect on your own servant leadership. Remember, we are all leaders in some capacity, whether in an organization, on a committee, in our families, or simply in our own lives. Can you provide an example of a time when you were a servant first and a leader second? What does it look like for you to lead by serving?

Read Mark 10:35–45. During the disciples' squabble over their need to be recognized and rewarded for their efforts, Jesus reminded them that they were to serve, just as he came to serve. Jesus understood a crucial truth: he "knew that the Father had put all things under his power, and that he had come from God and was returning to God" (John 13:3). Jesus derived his identity from his relationship with his Father and not from the opinions of his family and peers, in contrast to the disciples' desire to be recognized by the world.

Is your desire to be recognized as a servant by your family, friends, and co-workers, or is it to serve others as a result of your relationship with God? Take some time to journal your thoughts:

Spiritual Growth Plan Reflection

1. How are you currently serving others—not just volunteering your time, but truly working for the benefit of others with a genuine heart of servanthood?

2. What changes do you need to make in your schedule, your attitude, or your disposition so that that your relationship with God is guiding your service?

3. What changes do you need to make in what you are doing so that life becomes less about "paying your dues" and more about servant leadership?

Closing Prayer

3.6
HUMILITY

Read Genesis 3:5. Pride is the oldest sin in the Bible. In *The Life You've Always Wanted* (Grand Rapids: Zondervan, 2015), John Ortberg states that each of us has sought to take God's place ever since Adam and Eve did so in the garden of Eden. He identifies three features or aspects of the sin of pride:

- Pride involves vanity, a preoccupation with our own image or appearance.
- Pride involves stubbornness, which causes us to resist correction by others.
- Pride is a choice to exclude God and also other people from their proper place in our hearts; it destroys our ability to love.

Are you guilty of the sin of pride in any of its forms? Take a few minutes to journal about your pride and confess your pride to God:

The antidote to pride is humility. What is your definition of humility?

Read the following Bible passages and note what each says about what God expects from us:

- Luke 14:26:

- Matthew 19:21:

- John 14:15:

Read Micah 6:8. God requires humility of his people. How do the three previous passages explain to us how to develop and practice humility?

Read Philippians 2:5–8 and list the ways Jesus demonstrated humility:

John Maxwell identifies four major components of humility (see *Sometimes You Win, Sometimes You Learn* [London: Hodder Christian Books, 2013]):

1. *The heart of a servant.* How did the characters in each of the following passages demonstrate a servant's heart?

- 1 Samuel 26:8–11:

- Job 42:1–6:

- Genesis 50:15–21:

2. *A willingness to admit wrongdoing.* What do each of the following passages say about wrongdoing?

- 2 Samuel 12:13:

- Leviticus 4:22–23:

- Romans 8:5–8:

3. *A willingness to receive positive criticism.* Read Exodus 18:13–27. What advice did Moses receive? Accepting his father-in-law's advice demonstrated Moses' humility. What did it also prepare him to do?

4. *A reliance on God.* Read Exodus 14:13–14. What was Moses trying to get the Israelites to do?

Read Deuteronomy 8. What did God provide the Israelites as they wandered in the desert? What did Moses help the Israelites understand about their attitude?

Read the following Bible passages and note what each says about practicing humility:

- Matthew 11:28–30:

- Ephesians 5:21:

- 1 Peter 5:5–6:

- Colossians 3:12–13:

- James 3:13–14:

Spiritual Growth Plan Reflection

1. Reflect on struggles you have with any aspect of pride: vanity, stubbornness, and/or exclusion. How is a lack of humility impacting your relationship with God? with others?

2. Identify two or three steps you will take to develop and demonstrate humility.

Closing Prayer

3.7

THE TENSION OF TRUTH AND GRACE

How does God expect us to treat one another? Read each of the following Bible passages and note what instructions are provided for how we are to deal with others:

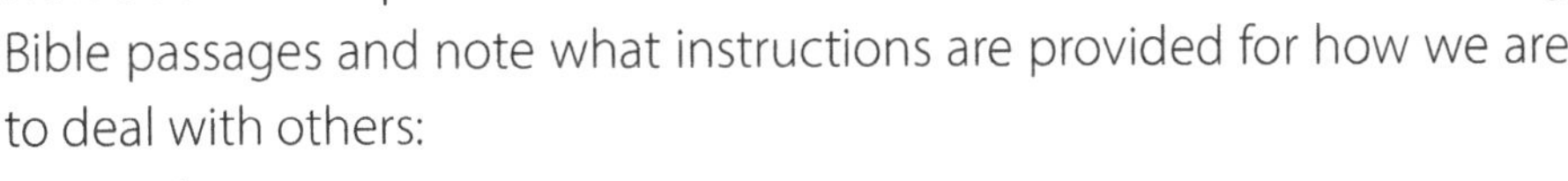

- Matthew 22:39:
- John 13:34:
- 1 John 4:7–11:
- Matthew 18:21–35:
- Ephesians 4:32:
- Colossians 3:12–15:

God also calls us to hold others accountable for living in the truth.

Read 2 Timothy 4:2. In what ways are we called to speak truth? What are the conditions we need to meet in order to speak truth to others?

Exhortation is the art of strongly urging someone to do the right things; to give warning or advice. In Galatians 6:1–5, Paul helped us understand how exhortation works. Read the passage and respond to the following:

- What is the purpose of exhortation?

- How should exhortation be approached?

- In verse 1 of the passage, Paul stated that "you who are spiritual" are qualified to exhort. What does this mean?

Read Galatians 5:19–21. Are the people described here qualified to exhort? Why or why not?

Now read Galatians 5:22–25. Why are the people described here qualified to exhort? What admonition is there for those who live by the Spirit (v 25)?

Speaking truth is not comfortable for most of us; there is always the chance the receiver of the advice and correction will respond unfavorably. Read Mark 6:14–29 for a story about a leader who responded badly. How did Herod react to John the Baptist's exhortation?

Now read 2 Samuel 12:13. How did King David respond to Nathan's rebuke?

The following passages provide some insight into appropriate truth-telling. What can be learned from each?

- Ephesians 4:15:
- Proverbs 15:31:
- Proverbs 27:6:

Part of the church's mission is to reach our community for Christ. As a church focused on reaching those who don't have a relationship with Jesus, we must be particularly sensitive to the tension between truth and grace. How do we balance truth and grace when sharing Christ with someone who isn't living a Christ-like life?

Read John 4:1–42 and answer the following questions:

- The fact that this person was a Samaritan and a woman made this encounter an unusual occurrence. What can we learn from the fact that Jesus approached a Samaritan woman?
- What balance between truth and grace was Jesus walking as he talked with the woman?
- What did Jesus try to teach his disciples through the encounter (see vv 31–38)?

- What was the end result of Jesus' encounter with the Samaritan woman (vv 39–42)?

Spiritual Growth Plan Reflection

1. Do you tend to respond to others more often with truth or with grace? Do you find it difficult to balance the two, to live in the tension? Journal your thoughts here:

2. What might God be trying to teach you about the tension between truth and grace?

3. How can you apply the example Jesus provided in John 4:1–42 to balancing truth and grace when interacting with those who don't have a relationship with Christ?

My Spiritual Growth Plan

The final activity in this study is developing a personal Spiritual Growth Plan. This plan should help you continue to strengthen your relationship with Christ and live a Christ-like life.

Use a blank sheet of paper to summarize the Spiritual Growth Plan Reflections from each week in the final segment of this study and share a copy with your group leader as a way of concluding the study:

1. Accountability, Integrity, and Financial Responsibility
2. Relational Integrity and Conflict Management
3. Confronting the Shadow Side
4. Sexual Integrity
5. Servanthood
6. Humility
7. The Tension of Truth and Grace